Hazardous
ANIMALS
of North-Western Australia

by Carolyn Thomson-Dans, Barbara York Main
and Kevin Crane

GW00691607

GOVERNMENT OF
WESTERN AUSTRALIA

Department of **Biodiversity,
Conservation and Attractions**

INTRODUCTION

The dangerous reputation of many of the animals described in this book is often most unfair. Most cases of injury occur when the animal is reacting defensively to what it perceives as an attack. It should be remembered that we share their territory and they may feel threatened by our presence.

Many of these creatures have fascinating life histories in their own right. They are usually very secretive and most species usually go out of their way to avoid people. You may be lucky enough to safely view some of them. If not, it is hoped that you will enjoy reading and learning about their amazing adaptations, feeding methods and defence mechanisms.

Venturing into the natural environment always involves some element of risk. If you go scuba diving on numerous occasions over a lengthy period, for instance, chances are that you will encounter a shark. However, this book provides suggestions on sensible precautions you can take to minimise the chances of such a meeting turning into a disaster. Most of these precautions are as simple as wearing strong footwear when walking in shallows or carrying a light at night to avoid inadvertently stumbling on a snake. Usually, the worst thing you can do is behave aggressively towards a dangerous animal. For instance, most people are bitten by snakes while trying to kill them. It should also be remembered that all of Western Australia's crocodiles and snakes are protected species.

The book also gives a brief outline of treatment in the event of an injury, but it should be stressed that readers should not rely on this advice alone. There are a number of other excellent publications available that provide a far more comprehensive outline of first aid.

With a little commonsense, you can enjoy the thrill of seeing a large crocodile, a snake or graceful stingray in the wild – from a safe distance.

Portugese man o'war on beach

SALTWATER CROCODILE

(*Crocodylus porosus*)

Their often massive size and ferocious nature has made them one of the most feared of all animals, but in the past the saltwater crocodile was hunted almost to extinction for its valuable skin. About 25,000 saltwater crocodiles are believed to have been harvested in WA between 1945 and 1970. Only 3,000 adults are estimated to remain and the species is now protected. Individuals are occasionally relocated to crocodile parks or farms if they are endangering public safety.

DESCRIPTION: The upper bodies of saltwater crocodiles are a mottled grey, brown or blackish colour. The snout is broader than that of the freshwater crocodile. They can reach up to seven metres, but individuals more than five metres long are rarely seen.

OTHER NAMES: Estuarine crocodile, 'saltie'.

DISTRIBUTION: Saltwater crocodiles inhabit the open ocean, seashores, mudflats, estuaries and rivers along the Kimberley coast and northern Pilbara. Their range once extended further south than this, but contracted significantly after extensive hunting mid last century. One vagrant was seen as far south as Shark Bay. Travellers in the Kimberley should be particularly wary following the wet season, as 'salties' can sometimes be found in rivers and gorges a considerable distance inland.

LIFE HISTORY: Youngsters feed on large marine invertebrates such as dragonflies and beetles. Adult crocodiles usually feed at night on fish, crustaceans, birds, mammals and reptiles such as turtles. During the wet season, females lay about 60 eggs in nests on riverbanks. They become especially aggressive while breeding. The temperature of the nest determines the sex of the young, with all the babies from a particular nest being entirely male or entirely female. Only two per cent of eggs, however, will survive. Crocodiles are superb hunters and are exceptionally fast on both land and

5

in the water. Ambush is a common tactic. They often submerge themselves near river banks, with only the nostrils exposed. When a kangaroo or other prey arrives to drink, the hunter will leap from the water with surprising agility and grab the unfortunate animal in its strong jaws. Because they have a small stomach and eat only once a week they often stow remaining meat underwater for later use.

PRECAUTIONS:

Seek reputable local advice about crocodiles before swimming, camping, fishing or boating and heed any warning signs.

There is potential danger anywhere saltwater crocodiles are found, including estuaries, tidal rivers, deep pools and mangrove shores. If in doubt, do not swim, canoe or use small boats.

Always watch out for large crocodiles. Children and pets are at particular risk in the water or at the water's edge.

Do not paddle, clean fish, prepare food or camp at the water's edge. Fill a bucket with water and do chores at least five metres from the water's edge. Returning regularly to the same spot is dangerous.

Don't lean over the edge of a boat, hang articles over the boat's edge or stand on logs overhanging water.

Stand at least a few metres back from the water's edge when fishing.

Dispose of food scraps, fish offal and other wastes away from your campsites, by burning it or taking it to the nearest official rubbish dump.

Never endanger the safety of others by stealing or damaging crocodile warning signs.

TREATMENT: Injury, blood loss and severe shock are the usual symptoms from crocodile attack. After removing the victim from the water a sufficient distance to prevent further attack, stop the bleeding by means of pressure and/or bandaging. Summon medical help and do not try to move the patient until aid arrives.

FRESHWATER CROCODILE

(*Crocodylus johnstoni*)

Unlike their larger relatives, freshwater crocodiles are not usually dangerous to people. They are very common in the Kimberley. Freshwater crocodiles are often seen basking in reasonable numbers around the perimeter of gorges and rivers, creating an interesting wildlife spectacle for visitors. These primitive reptiles have an ancient lineage and are remnants from the time of the dinosaurs.

DESCRIPTION: Freshwater crocodiles are grey or greenish-brown above, with heavily mottled flanks. In contrast to the saltwater variety, this species has a quite long, smooth and slender snout. However, they are often difficult to distinguish when partially submerged. They may reach up to three metres long.

OTHER NAMES: Johnstone's crocodile.

DISTRIBUTION: Freshwater crocodiles are widespread across northern Australia, including the Kimberley, Northern Territory and Queensland. They live largely in freshwater rivers, gorges and billabongs.

LIFE HISTORY: These reptiles are active by day but most hunting is done at night, when they search for fish, frogs and other small animals. They breed between October and November, at the end of the dry season, laying about 20 eggs in nests excavated in sandbanks. As with the saltwater crocodile, the sex of the young is determined by nest temperature. A steady temperature of 32 degrees Celsius results in the birth of males, but if the temperature fluctuates much above or below this, females result.

PRECAUTIONS: Never trail arms and legs from a boat in areas where freshwater crocodiles are known to live. A freshwater crocodile could easily mistake a small portion of your body as a fish or small animal. Do not approach them too closely, as a cornered freshwater crocodile will defend itself by biting with its razor-sharp teeth, scratching with its sharp claws or lashing with its long tail.

TAIPAN

(*Oxyuranus scutellatus*)

In WA, the taipan is found only in the far north Kimberley. It grows to about two metres long and has large fangs. It has been reputed to be Australia's most dangerous snake. However, relatively few people live near or visit its habitat, and they avoid humans, so it is rarely seen.

DESCRIPTION: The taipan varies from a glossy yellowish-brown to almost black in colour above and pale below. It has a distinct head that is paler than the body. Juveniles may be blotched. However, their colouration is highly variable. These reptiles may reach up to three metres long.

DISTRIBUTION: In WA, the taipan is largely confined to tropical, high rainfall areas, showing a preference for woodland and forest areas. It extends from the Mitchell Plateau south-west to Koolan Island. It also lives in the far north of the Northern Territory, northern and eastern Queensland and New Guinea.

LIFE HISTORY: Taipans are generally active by day, although they may be seen at night during periods of hot weather. Rodents are their favourite food, but they also hunt mammals as large as bandicoots, as well as birds and lizards. At other times they may shelter in hollow logs, rock heaps, old burrows and other refuges. They mate from July to December, when they are likely to be most aggressive. The females subsequently lay six to 25 eggs between October and February, which hatch after about two months. Hatchlings are about 60 centimetres long. They grow speedily and males may reach sexual maturity at only 16 months of age.

PRECAUTIONS: Avoid these animals at all times and do not attempt to kill them as they will defend themselves and strike, sometimes repeatedly, if harassed. They tend to be most active in the early morning and late afternoon.

KING BROWN

(*Pseudechis australis*)

Snakes have always captured our imagination, in part because of our morbid curiosity with all things dangerous. But they have fascinating lives in their own right and deserve to be studied and admired. The king brown is one of the most venomous snakes in Australia and is found throughout most of the State, particularly in the north. It tends to move off quietly when encountered, however it can be aggressive if angered and strikes rapidly.

DESCRIPTION: Adults are generally about two metres (the maximum recorded length is 2.75 metres) and have a brown to blackish-brown upper body and cream to salmon-coloured belly. However, the colour can be quite variable.

OTHER NAMES: Mulga snake.

DISTRIBUTION: The king brown is found throughout most of WA and the warmer regions of eastern Australia. It is absent from wetter areas across the southern coast. They live in a wide range of habitats, including heaths, open woodlands and deserts.

LIFE HISTORY: These creatures are mainly nocturnal, especially in northern areas, but are often seen during the day in cooler months, when they bask in morning sunlight on roads. They generally shelter in soil fissures, abandoned burrows and beneath debris. King brown snakes hunt small mammals, birds, frogs and reptiles, including other snakes. They reproduce by laying eggs, with hatchlings about 25 centimetres long. Clutches contain between 11 and 16 eggs.

PRECAUTIONS: Keep well clear of these fast-moving creatures. Always wear stout footwear in snake country and use a torch at night.

GWARDAR

(*Pseudonaja nuchalis*)

A close relative of the dugite, the gwardar appears in areas in which the dugite is absent.

DESCRIPTION: Gwardars are highly variable in colour. They are relatively slender. The upper scales vary from dark brown through orange to black, but the belly is whitish and has two often indistinct rows of small orange spots. Most individuals have a blackish mark on the neck, shaped like a V or W. Hatchlings may either display a herringbone pattern or have a uniform colour. Adults may also be slightly banded. They reach up to about 160 centimetres long.

OTHER NAMES: Western brown snake.

DISTRIBUTION: The gwardar is found throughout most of WA, with the exception of the south-western corner and the South Coast.

LIFE HISTORY: Gwardars are mainly active during the day, but can be nocturnal in warm weather. House mice are a favoured food source, so they are common near human dwellings and areas that have been disturbed. Gwardars also take a variety of other mammals and lizards and sometimes other snakes. The young, about 22 centimetres long, hatch from eggs laid in batches of up to 20. They shelter in holes in the ground and in hollow logs.

PRECAUTIONS: Keep well clear of this species, which will readily defend itself and is capable of striking at great speed. Do not try to kill them. Like all native animals, the species is protected and you also risk being bitten.

NORTHERN DEATH-ADDER
(*Acanthophis praelongus*)

This species and other death-adders have an ingenious method of luring prey. They will bury themselves in loose soil, leaves or other debris and wiggle the tip of the tail, which they position near the head. This lures lizards and other small animals. When such prey approaches close enough, the death-adder will suddenly strike.

DESCRIPTION: Death-adders have broad triangular heads, short stout bodies and worm-like tips on their tails, which may be cream, yellow or black. This species reaches up to a metre long, but is generally smaller. The head is distinctly wider than the neck.

DISTRIBUTION: They are found in a wide band across the northern half of Australia, covering most of the Kimberley region, and northern parts of the Northern Territory and Queensland. They also occur in southern New Guinea. They inhabit grasslands, woodlands and rocky ranges.

LIFE HISTORY: Death-adders are sluggish ambush hunters, so they have well-camouflaged bodies. This increases the chances of accidentally treading on them. This species gives birth to live young, with up to 20 in a litter. The newborn death-adders are about 40 centimetres long. Though they are mainly nocturnal, they may be encountered on warm nights. Their large fangs can deliver a powerful venom.

PRECAUTIONS: Always wear stout footwear and stay well away from these animals.

DESERT DEATH-ADDER

(*Acanthophis pyrrhus*)

In a similar manner to the northern death-adder, the desert death-adder will often bury itself in loose red sand and wiggle the tip of the tail so it looks like a tasty worm or caterpillar. This lures its prey of lizards and other small animals. The common name was originally deaf-adder, but over time it gradually evolved into death-adder. In fact, all snakes lack external ear openings but can detect low frequency sounds as vibrations.

DESCRIPTION: Death-adders have broad triangular heads, short robust bodies and markedly slender, cream, yellow or black tips on their tails. Their body colour varies from pale reddish-brown to rich red with yellowish cross bands. The undersides are creamy. This species reaches up to 76 centimetres long. The head is distinctly wider than the neck.

DISTRIBUTION: Desert death-adders are found throughout arid areas of western and central Australia. They are absent from the northern Kimberley. They generally inhabit hummock grasslands and rocky outcrops, sheltering under spinifex hummocks and in abandoned burrows.

LIFE HISTORY: These nocturnal creatures prey on small mammals and reptiles, especially lizards such as skinks and dragons. They give birth to 13 or so live young in each litter, each about 13 centimetres long. They are very hard to detect when they remain motionless.

PRECAUTIONS: Always wear stout footwear and stay well clear from these animals. Death-adders are sluggish and well-camouflaged, so could be trodden on accidentally. As their name suggests, they are dangerous.

HOW TO AVOID SNAKEBITES

- ❖ Wear stout footwear and long trousers.
- ❖ Make some noise as you move through the bush.
- ❖ Step up on logs before stepping over to check the area is clear.
- ❖ Use a torch at night.
- ❖ Don't try to kill or capture snakes.
- ❖ Don't put your hands into places you can't see, such as hollow logs.

Desert death adder

Photo – Brad Maryan

FIRST AID FOR SNAKEBITES

❖ Follow DRSABCD – Danger, Response, Send for help (call triple zero 000 for an ambulance), Airway, Breathing, CPR, Defibrillation.

❖ Ensure you are not in any danger from the snake.

❖ Rest and reassure the casualty.

❖ Do not wash the area. Immediately apply a broad, firm bandage around the limb to cover the bitten area. It should be as tight as one would bind a sprained ankle. As much of the limb should be bound up as possible. Crepe bandages are ideal but any flexible material can be used, such as clothing or old towels in strips. Note the time of bite and application of bandage.

❖ The limb must be kept as rigid as possible. Bind some type of splint to the limb – e.g. a piece of timber or another stiff object.

❖ Provide oxygen to the casualty if available. Do not elevate the pressure bandaged limb.

❖ Bring transport to the victim whenever possible. Do not let the casualty walk or run as this will increase the venom effect in the body.

❖ Leave the bandages and splint on until the patient has reached medical care but check circulation in fingers or toes.

❖ Do not cut or excise the bitten area.

❖ Arterial tourniquets are no longer recommended for snake bites.

❖ Do not take the snake with you, as the type of snake can be identified from the venom on the skin at the hospital.

SEA-SNAKES

For air-breathing animals, sea-snakes are remarkable divers. Some species can dive to 100 metres or more, and remain submerged for up to two hours. This may be partly due to the ability of some species to absorb part of the oxygen they need through their skins. Sea-snakes are adapted to breathe, feed, breed and grow in the sea.

DESCRIPTION: The 22 species of sea-snakes found in WA vary greatly in colour and markings. They all, however, have nostrils on the top of the snout, a boat-shaped abdomen and a flat tail which acts as a paddle to help them swim more effectively.

DISTRIBUTION: Most of these animals live in the warm, shallow seas of the tropics and sub-tropics. Some inhabit muddy estuaries, while others show a liking for clear waters near reefs. Individuals of some tropical species are occasionally swept south by warm currents, but eventually perish in the cooler southerly waters.

LIFE HISTORY: Sea-snakes give birth to live young at sea. The venom is used to subdue and kill prey, which is then grabbed in the jaws and swallowed whole. The skullbones of snakes are loosely attached and they can dislocate their lower jaws and slide them sideways to allowing them to swallow very large prey. They tend to be fussy eaters. Some only eat catfish, another the eggs of only two families of fish. Others dine on eels, fish, prawns, crabs and worms.

PRECAUTIONS: Although sea-snakes are highly venomous, they are placid and rarely attack people unless provoked and, even when they do, they do not always release venom. They are quite curious and may approach, but if you don't touch them they should leave you alone. Sea-snakes have been known to curl around divers' regulator hoses and limbs, especially during the breeding season. If this occurs, don't become alarmed, but wait patiently until they move off. Never touch sea-snakes washed onto beaches, even if they seem dead.

TREATMENT: If you are bitten, keep the injured limb still and seek immediate medical attention.

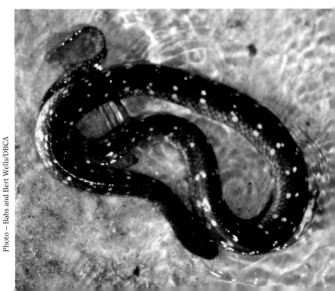

TIGER SHARK

(*Galeocerdo cuvier*)

Sharks have some amazing adaptations and the tiger shark is no exception. These instinctive creatures have the extraordinary ability to sense their prey by means of sensory receptors along the body. They can detect the slightest vibrations in the water. Other pores on the underside of the snout can detect small electric fields produced by all living animals, allowing them to locate flounders buried beneath the sand.

DESCRIPTION: Tiger sharks can grow up to six-and-a-half metres long and may be recognised by their size and the blunt snout. The young, known as pups, are born with distinctive stripes on their side, hence the fearsome name. These may be faint or missing from adults, generally fading in animals more than three metres long.

DISTRIBUTION: Tiger sharks are found in both coastal and offshore waters, often near reefs. They inhabit tropical and temperate seas throughout the world but in WA are rarely seen south of Jurien Bay.

LIFE HISTORY: Sharks are common inhabitants of our coastal waters. Tiger sharks give birth to live young. They have one of the largest litters of all sharks; 60 or more pups are produced, each measuring about 60 centimetres long.

PRECAUTIONS: Sharks are attracted to fish blood. To ensure they don't take too much interest in your activities, don't spear fish within their habitat or clean fish around swimming areas. While tiger sharks are regarded as dangerous, it is important not to panic or act provocatively if you see one.

TREATMENT: Injury, blood loss and severe shock are the usual symptoms from shark attack. After removing the victim from the water, the first consideration should be to stop the bleeding by means of pressure and/or bandaging. This is initially more important than seeking medical help. If the victim is wearing a wetsuit, leave it on. Call triple zero (000) for an ambulance, but do not move the patient further.

HAMMERHEAD SHARKS
(*Sphyrna* species)

Three species of hammerhead shark are found in north-western Australia but only one, the great hammerhead (*Sphyrna mokarran*), is considered dangerous. The scalloped hammerhead (*Sphyrna lewini*) and smooth hammerhead (*Sphyrna zygaena*) are quite timid and the similar-looking winghead shark (*Eusphyra blochii*) is considered harmless.

DESCRIPTION: The unusual shape of the head means that hammerheads can scan a wide area with their eyes, which are positioned at the end of each wing. The great hammerhead grows to about six metres long, while the scalloped and smooth hammerheads reach little more than four metres.

DISTRIBUTION: Hammerheads are found in tropical and temperate seas throughout the world, in both coastal and offshore waters. The smooth hammerhead is found around the entire coast of WA, but the great hammerhead and smooth hammerhead are rarely seen south of the Abrolhos.

LIFE HISTORY: Hammerheads are sociable creatures and in some areas swim in packs of between 10 and 20. In south-eastern Australia they have been reported in groups of up to 200. Hammerheads commonly produce litters of up to 40 pups, born with the 'wings' on their head folded back.

PRECAUTIONS: Don't spear fish within their habitat or clean fish around swimming areas. They are less likely to attack people in groups of two or more. Swimmers and divers are also advised not to thrash around in the water, urinate in the water or swim with bleeding wounds. If a dangerous shark is seen, abandon any caught fish and immediately leave the area without making any jerky movements.

Smooth hammerhead

TREATMENT: Remove the victim from the water to prevent further attack or drowning and immediately stem the flow of blood by applying direct pressure or bandaging before seeking medical help. If the victim is wearing a wetsuit, leave it on. Call an ambulance and do not move the patient further.

Rays are among the most graceful animals that inhabit our underwater world. Most have venomous spines attached to the tail. The venom of some species, such as the black stingray (*Dasyatus thetis*), is particularly potent, and can affect the circulatory system and cause heart failure. The ornate numbfish (*Hypnos westraliensis*) and the numbfish (*H. monopterygium*) have organs along their backs that can give a powerful electric shock if they are handled or accidentally trodden on, but this in itself is not life-threatening.

DESCRIPTION: All rays have flat bodies. The tail varies from quite thick to thin and rodent-like. Some such as eagle rays have pointed wings, whereas others appear rounded from above. Numbfish have rounded bodies and ornate numbfish are shaped like flattened tadpoles. Rays are usually coloured to blend in well with their surroundings.

DISTRIBUTION: Rays are distributed throughout the world in a variety of habitats but they are usually bottom-dwellers.

LIFE HISTORY: Like sharks, to which they are closely related, rays do not have true bones but cartilage and have an ancient lineage that can be traced back 350 million years. As with many shark species, almost all types of rays hatch their eggs within the uterus and then give birth to live young. They emerge tail-first and their venom spines are rubbery at birth, presumably to prevent the mother being impaled. The manta rays found in tropical waters are large and powerful and also have a reputation for being dangerous, but they are harmless plankton feeders.

PRECAUTIONS: Rays are usually not aggressive, but it is best to admire them from a distance. Wear exposure suits, gloves and suitable footwear when snorkelling and diving and shuffle, rather than stride, when in shallows.

TREATMENT: If perforated by a spine, hot water may relieve the intense pain usually experienced. Be sure to test the water

Above: Numbfish   Below: Cowtail stingray

to make sure it is as hot (but not hotter) than the rescuer can tolerate before placing in the casualty's affected area. Always seek medical attention, even if the injury does not appear to be serious. People given a shock by numbfish may be at risk of drowning if temporarily disabled. However, treatment is usually not needed.

CATFISH

Named because of their whiskers, catfish have also evolved venomous spines for protection against predators. Unfortunately, they may inadvertently cause painful and sometimes serious injuries to people if trodden on. These creatures lurk around the shallows of estuaries, rivers, beaches and mudflats but generally go out of their way to avoid swimmers. However, some injuries take place when people tread on dead or injured animals.

DESCRIPTION: Numerous species of catfish are found in north-western Australia. Some species grow to more than a metre long, but most are smaller. There is usually a prominent dorsal fin which conceals one of the three spines. The other two are hidden in the pectoral fins. Depending on the species, the tail is either long and tapering, or forked, as in the giant salmon catfish.

OTHER NAMES: Cobbler.

DISTRIBUTION: Catfish inhabit fresh or salt water around the entire coast of WA and elsewhere.

LIFE HISTORY: The unusual whiskers of catfish are used to sense potential food under the sand. The venomous glands are at the base of the spine.

PRECAUTIONS: Never handle a catfish, take care when hauling in fishing nets or lines and avoid walking in shallows without protective footwear. Do not throw dead or injured fish back into shallows where they could be a hazard to others.

TREATMENT: Intense pain and shock are common symptoms. Catfish have even caused death on rare occasions. Hot water is an effective means of treating the symptoms – be careful that the water is only as hot as the casualty can bear. Be prepared to give further first aid if respiratory or cardiovascular problems are experienced. Children are at greater risk than adults. Surgery may be needed to remove the barbed spines. Aboriginal people used the masticated leaves of the freshwater mangrove (*Barringtonia acutangula*) as an ointment around the wound.

Hyrtyl tandan catfish

ESTUARINE STONEFISH

(*Synanceja horrida*)

Stonefish inhabit coastal reefs and shallow mudflats and usually lie on the sea floor, partially buried in sand. The body exudes a sticky slime that seaweed and other material will adhere to, as a further aid to camouflage. If people tread on this animal the sharp, venomous spines can pierce their feet, causing severe pain and tissue damage. The spines can even penetrate sandshoes.

DESCRIPTION: These fish look just like rocks, especially as they remain remarkably still for long periods. They have warty projections on their dull greyish-brown body and large pectoral fins, used to dig into sandy hiding places. They have tiny eyes and a large, almost vertical mouth. These unlovable animals may reach up to 47 centimetres long.

OTHER NAMES: Rockfish, devilfish, goblinfish.

DISTRIBUTION: Estuarine stonefish are found around the top two-thirds of the Australian coast, from Moreton Bay in Queensland to the Abrolhos Islands in WA.

LIFE HISTORY: Stonefish capture prey by stealth, concealing themselves in sand and sucking small fish swimming past into their large mouth. The mouth operates almost like a vacuum cleaner. They gulp in the water containing the unwary prey with remarkable speed, then eject the water through their gills. The speed with which they strike has been timed photographically at just 0.015 seconds. They sometimes give chase over short distances.

PRECAUTIONS: Always wear strong footwear (not thongs) when walking in shallows from Shark Bay northwards, and tread gently. Never touch a stonefish.

TREATMENT: Stonefish can cause excruciating pain, severe shock, nausea and other symptoms, even, on rare occasions, death. Since an antivenom was isolated in the 1950s no-one has died from stonefish wounds in Australia. The pain can be relieved by bathing in hot water. There may be long-term complications. Anyone with the bad luck to be stung should seek medical attention.

Above: Head of a stonefish   Below: Stonefish dorsal spines

BUTTERFLY COD

The butterfly cod is a spectacular animal with brilliant colouring and long defensive spiny fins. It is part of the scorpionfish family, but unlike other members of this family, which often rely on camouflage for protection, it swims freely around coral reefs, leaving its venomous fins to give it 360-degree protection.

DESCRIPTION: Butterfly cod are characterised by their long, spiny fins. The dorsal, anal and pelvic fins are all venomous. These brightly-coloured fish grow up to 30 centimetres long.

OTHER NAMES: Firefish (*Pterois* sp.), lionfish (*Dendrochirus* sp.), zebrafish.

DISTRIBUTION: Butterfly cod are predominantly found in tropical and subtropical waters. Smaller animals may be seen in temperate waters due to larvae getting caught in currents, but usually don't survive the cooler winter months.

LIFE HISTORY: Butterfly cod are nocturnal animals, becoming active when the sun sets. During the day they are mostly stationary. They show little fear of divers and often orientate their body so that their dorsal fins point forward in a defensive pose. They feed mostly on crustaceans but may consume fish including juveniles of their own species.

PRECAUTIONS: Butterfly cod are not aggressive. The long venomous spines are purely defensive. Injury prevention is simple: don't run into these animals. Stay at least a metre away when observing them, so you are not putting yourself at risk. Show some respect to these beautiful animals and they will leave you alone.

TREATMENT: Wounds from the spines of butterfly cod can result in unbelievable agony. The injured limb should be placed in water as hot as can be tolerated to help alleviate the pain. Immediate medical aid is recommended, as a local anaesthetic may be needed for the pain.

Above: Juvenile lionfish   Below: Zebra lionfish

MORAY EELS

Because of its ferocious appearance, the moray eel has long had a fearsome reputation. Roman legend tells of Nero throwing slaves into watery pits filled with moray eels so bored aristocrats could gain pleasure from seeing people eaten alive. While it is a reputation that moray eels find hard to live down, they are not aggressive animals and will attack only when threatened. At least 15 different species live in north-western Australia.

DESCRIPTION: The long slender snake-like body, combined with a large set of jaws, sends shivers down the spine of many who encounter a moray eel. Most species have long, sharp canine teeth but some do have low, nodular teeth. Morays are usually one to two metres long, though some will reach up to three metres long and 30 centimetres in diameter. Colour varies from black to brownish-yellow with a pale underside.

DISTRIBUTION: Moray eels are found in tropical and temperate waters throughout the world.

LIFE HISTORY: These creatures live in holes in the reef. They rarely venture far from these crevices and feed by concealing themselves in the reef and waiting for an unwary meal to swim by. The morays with long, canine teeth feed mainly on fish and occasionally on octopuses and crustaceans. Other species with blunt, crushing teeth prey principally on crustaceans, especially crabs. Individuals nearly always have their mouths open and appear ready to bite. In fact, the mouth is open to allow water to pass through the gills, enabling them to breathe.

PRECAUTIONS: If a moray eel attacks, it is difficult to grasp and its muscular jaws can clamp with great power. Even if the eel can be dislodged, it may resume attack. Most attacks occur when divers accidentally bump into an eel they have not seen or venture too close. To avoid this, divers should always maintain proper buoyancy so they are swimming just above the reef, a habit which also safeguards delicate corals. Spearing these animals is another

Photos – Takamasa Tonozuka/Lochman Transparencies

sure way to have a very annoyed moray eel attached to your leg. Feeding eels is strongly discouraged, as it has the potential to make eels seeking food aggressive towards divers.

TREATMENT: Slashing lacerations can be expected if bitten by a moray eel. The more severe the bite, the deeper and more potentially dangerous the lacerations will be. The immediate problem after an attack is blood loss. Direct pressure should be applied to the wound with anything available and then preferably with a bandage. If the bite is not severe and the bleeding under control, medical aid is still advised, as secondary infection in the wound is common.

PORTUGUESE MAN O'WAR

(*Physalia* species)

Remarkably, Portuguese men o'war are not solitary animals but colonies formed of numerous creatures living together as a single entity. Their bobbing 'float' at the surface can be spotted from some distance away. These resemble blue bottles, hence the alternative common name. They are occasionally seen in their thousands.

DESCRIPTION: Each man o'war has numerous dense shorter tentacles beneath the float and a single coiled tentacle that may reach seven metres long. They are a vivid blue.

OTHER NAMES: Bluebottle.

DISTRIBUTION: These stinging creatures live right around the Australian coastline.

LIFE HISTORY: Portuguese men o'war drift along the surface of our oceans feeding on small fish and other animals. These are paralysed by the trailing tentacles. The shorter tentacles are then used to tie the prey to the bottom of the float, where it is slowly devoured. People unfortunate enough to be stung experience severe pain and lacerations, which will gradually ease. Aching may last for a day or more.

PRECAUTIONS: Avoid blue bobbing floats in the water and do not touch men o'war stranded on the beach.

TREATMENT: Do not use vinegar on a Portuguese man o'war sting. Remove the tentacles if you can, then use a cold compress (icepack) to relieve pain and swelling by reducing the flow of blood to the injured area. Severe stings can result in fainting, cramps, nausea and breathing difficulties. Seek immediate medical attention if someone is particularly allergic and be ready to provide cardiopulmonary resuscitation if necessary.

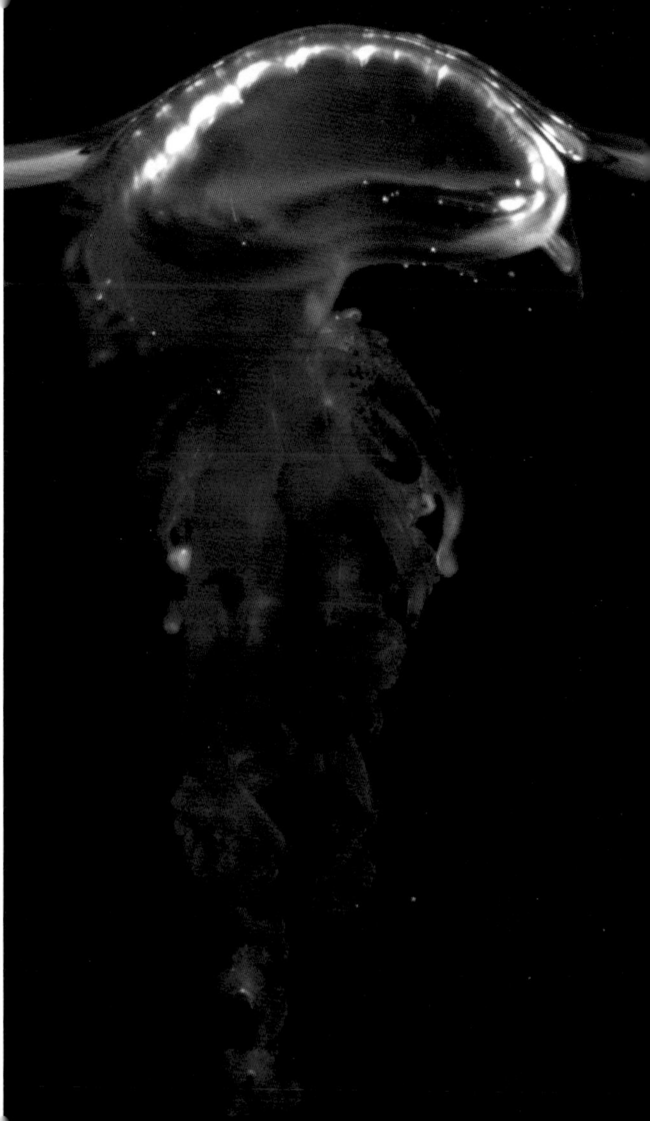

Photo – Clay Bryce/Lochman Transparencies

BOX JELLYFISH

(*Chironex fleckeri*)

This highly dangerous animal inhabits tropical and sub-tropical Australian waters. It is the largest box jellyfish; its squarish round-topped bell can reach the size of a human head and weigh more than six kilograms. It is one of the most venomous jellyfish and its sting can kill. Its sticky tentacles contain millions of individual stinging cells called nematocysts which discharge a potent toxin that paralyses and soon kills the victim.

DESCRIPTION: These transparent animals are difficult, if not impossible, to see in the water. The bell has a box-like shape with 15 to 20 tentacles, each up to three metres long, hanging from each corner.

OTHER NAMES: Sea wasp.

PREFERRED HABITAT: Box jellyfish prefer sediment-clouded coastal waters, such as those around the mouths of rivers and creeks. They are most common on calm, overcast days in summer and early autumn, but may be found at any time of year. Fortunately, they avoid clear waters around coral reefs and offshore islands.

LIFE HISTORY: The box jellyfish uses rivers and estuaries to reproduce. Eggs settle on the underside of rocks and develop from a polyp to a free-swimming medusa. The juveniles are flushed out of the estuaries with the onset of the wet season and mature in three to four months. The powerful toxin prevents heartbeat and breathing, and can damage red blood cells and skin tissue. Excruciating pain will be experienced on contact, followed by collapse and breathing problems. In severe cases, death can occur in less than three minutes.

PRECAUTIONS: Wear exposure suits when swimming or diving in northern waters. Avoid entering the water if box jellyfish have been reported in the area, regardless of the time of year.

TREATMENT: If someone is stung, pour domestic vinegar over the

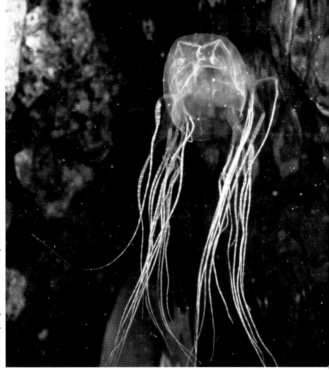

Photo – Clay Bryce/Lochman Transparencies

tentacles and the area of the sting, then carefully remove the tentacles (without directly touching them). Vinegar deactivates the discharge of nematocysts (stinging cells) of all known members of the box jellyfish group and so prevents further injection of venom. Do not use fresh water to wash away the tentacles as it will cause the undischarged nematocysts to fire. If you don't have access to vinegar use seawater. Always seek immediate medical attention. Keep the casualty at rest and be prepared to give CPR until help arrives.

BLUE-RINGED OCTOPUS

(*Hapalochlaena* species)

These remarkable and spectacular creatures deliver a warning before they bite. When irritated or disturbed they rapidly develop brilliant blue rings. In such cases, you should admire their colourful appearance from a safe distance. At least three species of blue-ringed octopus live off northern Australia. They are extremely venomous and, although such cases are rare, can cause human death.

DESCRIPTION: Blue-ringed octopus are no more than 20 centimetres long. They are normally well-camouflaged, with yellow, brown and grey bodies. There are dark brown blotches and bands on the arms.

PREFERRED HABITAT: They live under rocks and dead coral, on reef flats and in tidal pools in muddy areas.

LIFE HISTORY: The name octopus comes from the word Octopoda, meaning 'eight-footed'. All octopus have eight arms. They are molluscs and, along with their close relatives the squids and cuttlefish, are the most highly-developed invertebrates, with a well-developed brain and eye structure. They hide themselves in rocks and other debris and in crevices. Most octopus have short lives and only live for about a year. Blue-ringed octopus kill their prey with a potent toxin injected with their bite. People who are bitten suffer paralysis and respiratory failure.

PRECAUTIONS: Be cautious when handling dead shells or discarded cans and bottles and when exploring underwater crevices or caverns.

TREATMENT: The bite does not cause pain and puncture marks may not be visible. Numbness will be experienced and it may become difficult to speak or see. If bitten, keep the casualty calm and the injured limb still. Apply a pressure immobilisation bandage and splint the bandaged limb. Blue-ringed octopus venom causes muscle paralysis leading to breathing failure so seek urgent medical aid and be prepared to give cardiopulmonary resuscitation until help arrives. Paralysis is long lasting but it will eventually abate.

Photo – Clay Bryce/Lochman Transparencies

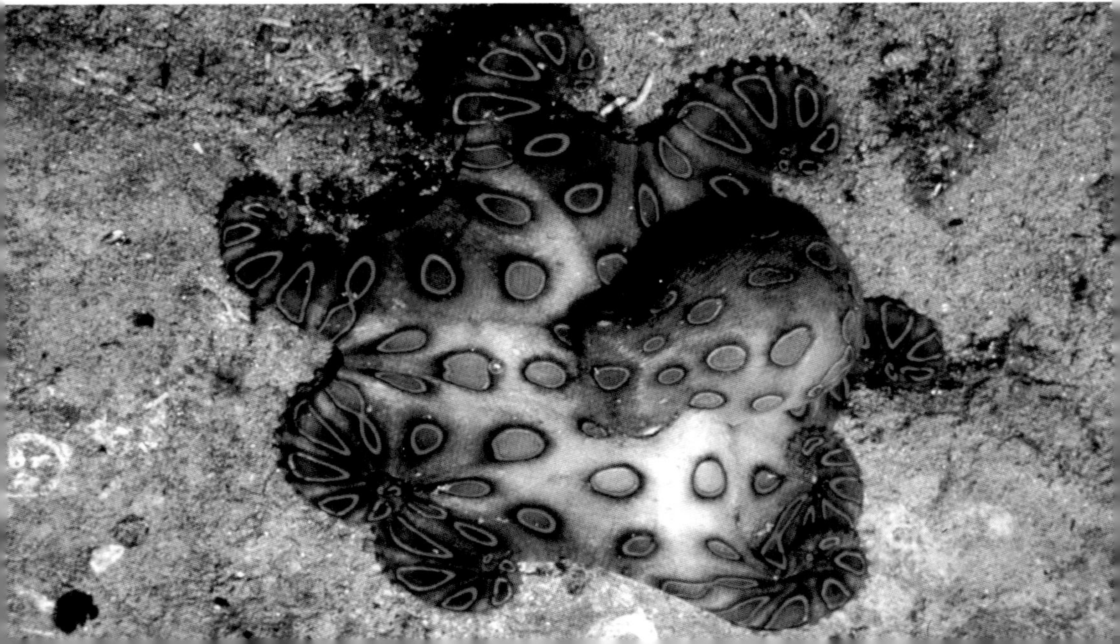

CONESHELLS

Coneshells may bury themselves in sand, with only their snorkel-like siphon extended. Some are reported to shoot out their harpoon-like teeth like a dart or they may leap out to stab a fast-moving fish. A number of these detachable teeth are stored inside the body ready for use. The powerful venom injected with the barb paralyses the prey and the coneshell proceeds to devour its meal. Eight species of coneshell in northern Australia are known to be or thought to be poisonous. However, these nocturnal animals are rarely seen and usually only bite in self-defence, when people are trying to remove a live animal for its beautiful shell.

DESCRIPTION: Coneshells are attractive animals, with conical or cylindrical shells. The huge number of species (more than 300) are found in a great variety of decorative patterns and vary greatly in size. Live coneshells have a siphon that protrudes through a notch at the pointed end of the shell, just above the head. Beneath is a stalk tipped with a single eye and a snout-like feeding organ that holds a venomous barb. Depending on the species, coneshells may reach up to 10 centimetres long.

DISTRIBUTION: Coneshells are largely animals of tropical areas.

LIFE HISTORY: By day coneshells bury themselves in sand and usually emerge at night in search of small fish, snails or worms. The siphon is used to suck water into the body. As well as passing through the gills, the water is transported over an organ used to detect chemicals in the water that reveal the presence of potential prey.

PRECAUTIONS: While not all coneshells are dangerous, it is far better to be wary of all species. The proboscis from which the poison harpoons are shot can become very long very quickly, striking a finger regardless of where the animal is held. Avoid live coneshells, regardless of the species.

TREATMENT: Symptoms vary with the species, but include numbness, swelling, pain, progressive paralysis and, in the case of the Geographer cone (*Conus geographus*), even death.

You should immobilise the bitten area with a bandage and splint and seek immediate medical attention. Be prepared to provide cardiopulmonary resuscitation to the victim if breathing failure appears likely and continue until help arrives or paralysis abates.

FIRE CORALS

(*Millepora* species)

Although fire coral looks similar to coral, the name is a misnomer as it actually belongs to the same group of animals as stinging hydroids. Fire coral can cause highly painful wounds.

DESCRIPTION: There are about 48 species of fire coral recorded and these often have a large diversity of growth forms. Some are only small encrusting corals, while others have many fused vertical plates or column-like projections. In addition to this, the same species may have different growth forms at different depths in response to the availability of light. Colour also varies from white to yellow to greenish-grey.

DISTRIBUTION: Fire corals are found in warmer tropical and subtropical waters. In Australia, they range from the northern and central Great Barrier Reef and Coral Sea on the east coast and south to North West Cape on the west coast.

LIFE HISTORY: Fire corals extend their polyps into the water column to feed. They rely on water currents to wash small particles of food past their waiting mouths. Unlike true corals, fire coral has separate feeding polyps, surrounded by smaller stinging polyps. The stinging polyps stun the prey as it swims past and pass it to the feeding polyps.

PRECAUTIONS: Most interactions with fire coral occur when unwary divers accidentally brush a dangling hand over the coral. To avoid this, divers should always maintain proper buoyancy so they are swimming just above the reef.

TREATMENT: Divers touching fire coral will experience sharp, burning pain in the affected area. The severity of the sting depends on the area of skin that has brushed against the coral, and sensitive skin will experience a more severe reaction. Red swelling and welts may develop. Severe stings can result in fainting, cramps and nausea. While symptoms should subside with time, medical aid may be required in severe cases.

STINGING HYDROIDS

Hydroids are closely related to corals and jellyfish and possess similar stinging cells to subdue their prey. Hydroids, however, have a delicate fern-like appearance and can be easily mistaken for seaweed.

DESCRIPTION: Two species of hydroids have a nasty sting. *Lytocarpus philipinnus* is the more beautiful of the two, with many delicate white fronds arising from a single base. *Aglaophenia cupressina* is a brownish-green colour and is easy to mistake for a brown seaweed. It grows in clumps, with the fronds up to 15 centimetres long.

DISTRIBUTION: Hydroids are found in both tropical and temperate waters around the world. Both species of stinging hydroids are found in north-western Australia and can be seen as far south as Perth.

LIFE HISTORY: Being carnivores which are permanently attached to reefs and other underwater structures, hydroids rely on water currents to wash food particles past them. As a result, they are most abundant where there is a good supply of water-borne food. Hence reefs in fast-flowing tidal channels and places where water is channelled through gaps in the reef usually support high numbers of hydroids.

PRECAUTIONS: Most interactions with stinging hydroids occur when divers accidentally brush a dangling hand over the animal. To avoid this, divers should always maintain proper buoyancy so they are swimming just above the reef. Exposure suits are recommended when diving or snorkelling.

TREATMENT: Divers touching stinging hydroids will experience sharp burning pain in the affected area. The severity of the sting will increase with the area of skin brushing the hydroid and will also be more severe on sensitive skin. Red swelling and welts may develop. If part of the animal is on the skin, vinegar can be used to ease the pain. Severe stings can result in fainting, cramps and nausea. Symptoms should subside with time, but medical aid may be required in severe cases.

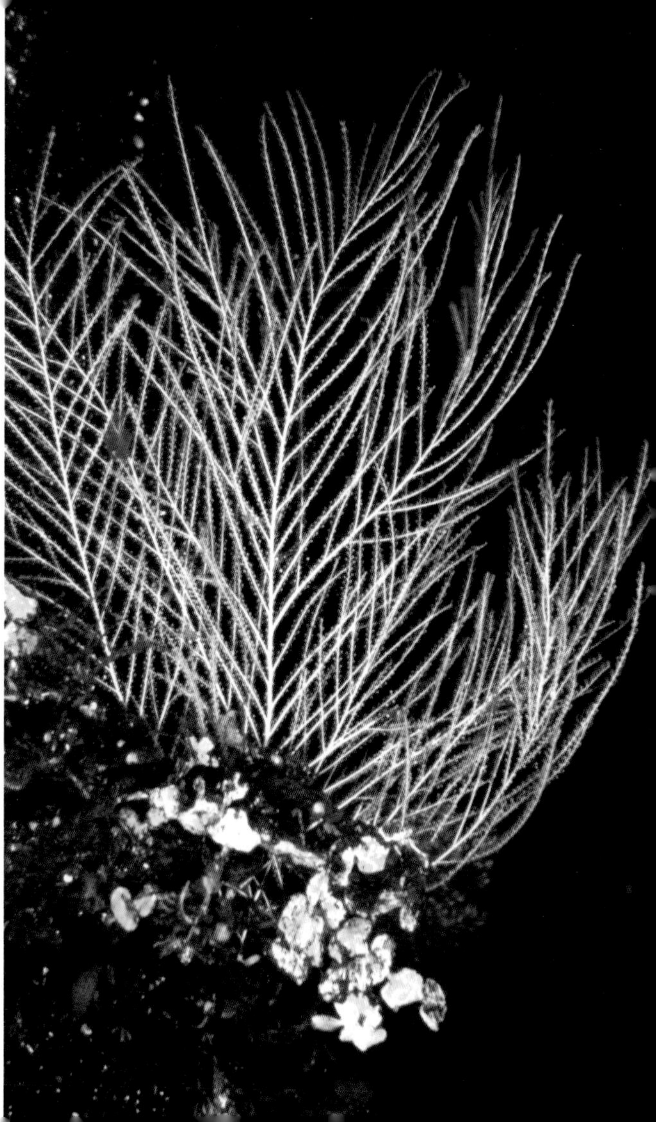

Photo – Takamasa Tonozuka/Lochman Transparencies

REDBACK SPIDER

(*Latrodectus hasselti*)

The redback spider is firmly embedded in Australian bush lore and culture. Once greatly feared because of its venom, it is not now regarded as such as danger because of the availability of an anti-venene.

DESCRIPTION: The body of an adult female spider is about the size and shape of a pea, shiny black with a red stripe on the back and a red hourglass pattern underneath. The legs are long, spindly and spineless. Young females and male spiders are creamy coloured, with darker streaks, and the red stripe and hourglass pattern is paler than in adults.

DISTRIBUTION, HABITAT AND WEB: Redback spiders are found throughout Australia, especially in drier regions. In northern WA they are more abundant around settlements than in the bush. Spiders are readily carried about on vehicles. This species lives within a permanent, tangly, very tough cobweb used to trap insects. The web always has contact with the ground. In the bush, webs may be in logs, under stones or at the butts of shrubs or under dry cliff faces and cave openings. Around buildings, they shelter against fences, under furniture, in tins and boxes. Outside toilets are a favourite spot.

LIFE HISTORY: Spiders mature in the spring and early summer. The males cluster in female webs and are eaten after mating. Females produce about four or more marble-sized yellowish egg cocoons. The tiny, black-spotted creamy spiderlings disperse aerially in the autumn, before settling and making individual webs.

SYMPTOMS AND TREATMENT: Care should be taken when moving about in likely haunts of the redback spider, especially in the outback when medical help may not be close by. While the bite itself may not be painful, the symptoms are. These include intense local pain which increases and spreads, headache, muscle weakness or spasms, abdominal pain and nausea and vomiting.

Profuse sweating, which may cause dehydration, is also a common symptom. Apply a cold pack to the bitten area to lessen the pain and seek immediate medical attention.

HUNTSMAN SPIDER

(*Heteropoda renibulbis*)

This and some other species of huntsman spider in northern WA are large and aggressive. Although they are poisonous and there are cases of hospitalisation, the spiders are not known to be highly venomous. However, they are capable of giving a painful bite because of their size (they have a leg span of about 15 centimetres) and strong fangs.

DESCRIPTION: This species of huntsman spider has a large, flat and crab-like body with all its legs turned frontwards. It can also run sideways. The body and legs are greyish-brown and mottled.

DISTRIBUTION AND HABITAT: It is found throughout the Kimberley region, especially in coastal rainforest patches, and across northern Australia, living in tree trunks and frequently among boulders. Similar species occur further south in the Pilbara region of WA.

BEHAVIOUR: These spiders are nocturnal, emerging at night to hunt and feed, mainly on large insects. They remain stationary, flattening the body with legs spread out on rocks or bark, waiting for passing prey rather than stalking it. If disturbed, they may become aggressive, and attack with front legs raised, or they may scuttle quickly away.

PRECAUTIONS: Use a torch when moving about the bush at night, and do not rest your hands on rocks or tree trunks without first looking carefully. If you are camping out, sleep inside a mosquito net, and do not leave your bedding open as a spider may be encouraged to join you before you retire. If you are bitten, a cold pack will help relieve pain.

BIRD-EATING SPIDERS

(*Selenocosmia* species)

Although commonly given the fearsome name of 'bird-eating' spiders, Australian examples of this group feed mainly on insects and only occasionally on small vertebrates, mainly frogs and lizards. They belong to the trapdoor and funnelweb group of spiders, which are technically called Mygalomorphae – the word 'mygale' referring to the furry appearance of a field mouse. There are several species in north-western Australia. Some occur in rainforest patches and *Selenocosmia stirlingi* is widely distributed through the whole of the interior arid country. There are cases of bites causing illness and at least one instance of a dog fatality.

DESCRIPTION: Bird-eating spiders are very large. With their legs spread apart they would easily cover a saucer. They are extremely hairy and dark brown in colour and their very long fangs are parallel and bite downwards like a snake.

BEHAVIOUR AND BURROW: All species dig a very deep, sinuous burrow, which may be more than a metre long. A mesh of web may be spread outside the entrance to ensnare prey, and the spiders will also chase insects which come near the hole. Mating is usually associated with the wet season, when males abandon their burrows to search for female nests. These 'wandering' males are sometimes encountered by people. If provoked, they may be very aggressive.

PRECAUTIONS: Use a torch when outside at night, especially just before and after rain. Wear stout footwear. If you see a spider, do not annoy it. If bitten seek immediate medical aid and use a cold pack to reduce the pain.

DOUBLE-DOORED TRAPDOOR SPIDER

(*Missulena pruinosa*)

There are several species of *Missulena* in northern WA, but the double-doored trapdoor spider is confined to rainforest habitats of the Kimberley and Northern Territory. Other species are found in drier country. These animals are also commonly known as mouse spiders. While they are known to be venomous, most cases of bites have not caused illness.

DESCRIPTION: Female spiders are squat and thickset, with short, stumpy legs. They are usually black. The body (head and abdomen) of an adult is about the size of a 20 cent coin. The head is very high and slopes steeply behind the eyes, which are small and spread across the front. Male spiders are smaller than females and have longer, thinner legs. The male of *Missulena pruinosa* has a white patch on the back of the abdomen, whereas males of some inland species are brightly-coloured, with a red head and 'jaws' and a blue abdomen.

BEHAVIOUR AND BURROW: The burrow usually has two doors at the entrance. However, burrows are well camouflaged and in remote rainforest patches so they are rarely seen. At night, female spiders may hunt a few centimetres from the burrow and people may therefore come across them on the surface. Male spiders leave their burrows when searching for females with which to mate and, unlike most other species of trapdoor spider, male *Missulena* spiders often wander during the day time. If encountered they become very aggressive, raise their front legs and open the fangs widely.

PRECAUTIONS: Never meddle with these spiders. If bitten, and symptoms of discomfort or illness develop, seek medical attention.

GREEN TREE ANT

(*Oecophylla smaragdina*)

Green tree ants are found right across humid, tropical Australia in open forest and along the edges of rainforests. Aboriginal people used them as bush tucker. They would eat the abdomen and make a drink out of the nest. Although they are not dangerous like bulldog ants (*Myrmecia* species) they can cause considerable discomfort, especially if a lot of ants attack at the same time. They exude formic acid onto their bite which causes a stinging sensation.

DESCRIPTION: These medium-sized ants are mostly green.

BEHAVIOUR: Green tree ants weave gum leaves or other broad leaves together into hollow nests (like a small paper bag). Lines of ants forage away from the nest. Nests usually contain large numbers of ants and if the nest is knocked the ants are likely to swarm out. A spider (*Amyciaea albomaculata*) mimics the green tree ant and preys upon them. They are sometimes seen dangling on a thread with an ant clasped in their fangs.

PRECAUTIONS: Wear a hat with a brim and a shirt with long sleeves and a collar. Never deliberately touch a nest. To ensure a comfortable night's sleep, do not set up a sleeping bag under tree branches bearing nests.

TICKS, INCLUDING KANGAROO TICKS
(*Acarina* species)

There are several species of ticks, both 'hard' and 'soft', which can cause discomfort to people. Ticks belong to the same group as spiders and scorpions (arachnids). However, the head and abdomen are fused into one body piece. Ticks are blood suckers, and the mouth parts are in the form of a proboscis with backward directed hooks. Thus they are very difficult to remove. The paralysis tick, common on the east coast of Australia, is not known to occur in WA. However, other ticks can cause allergic reactions as well as persistent itchy lumps.

PRECAUTIONS: Do not sit on or disturb the ground where kangaroos have been resting (kangaroo 'squats'), as ticks shelter here in the soil between feeds. Squats are bare, slightly scuffed patches of soil under the shade of shrubs or low trees (pellets of kangaroo dung may also be present).

TREATMENT: Carefully remove ticks by grasping the proboscis with tweezers and pulling sharply. Do not squeeze the body as this will force the toxins back into the victim. Part of the proboscis may break off in the skin and cause an itchy lump. Another technique is to put methylated spirits or kerosene on the body of the tick, which should then come out. If seriously inconvenienced, seek medical attention.

Opposite: Kangaroo tick

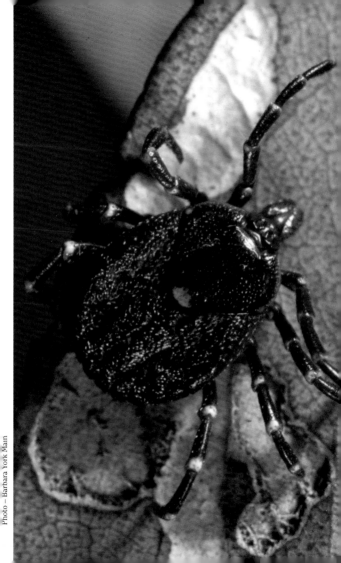

SIGHTING RECORD

SPECIES	DATE	LOCALITY
saltwater crocodile		
freshwater crocodile		
taipan		
king brown		
gwardar		
northern death-adder		
desert death-adder		
sea-snake		
tiger shark		
hammerhead shark		
stingrays and numbfish		
catfish		
estuarine stonefish		
butterfly cod		
moray eel		
Portuguese man o'war		
box jellyfish		
blue-ringed octopus		
coneshell		
fire coral		
stinging hydroid		
redback spider		

SIGHTING RECORD		
SPECIES	**DATE**	**LOCALITY**
huntsman spider		
bird-eating spider		
double-doored trapdoor spider		
green tree ant		
ticks		

Hammerhead shark

INDEX

20180034 0618 5M